ALFRED's SACRED PERFORMER COLLECTIONS

Sunday Morning *Praise Companion*

33 Favorite Contemporary Worship Selections

Arranged by Victor Labenske

At my church, there are two worship services: the Classic Service is traditional, and the Celebration Service is contemporary. This book has given me the opportunity to arrange favorite songs of both congregations, though the collection emphasizes the music of the second service. In this volume of the Sunday Morning Companion series, I have tried to capture the exuberance of contemporary worship with a wide variety of popular sacred music. The arrangements are accessible to intermediate and late-intermediate pianists and are also useful for advanced pianists who need to learn music quickly for use in church. I hope that with these arrangements pianists will experience, as I did, a wide range of worship experiences—from joyful excitement to pensive contemplation. May God bless you with an inspiring music ministry!

Victor Labenske

ABOVE ALL 2

ALL WHO ARE THIRSTY 5

AMAZING GRACE (MY CHAINS ARE GONE) . . 8

BEAUTIFUL ONE 12

BETTER IS ONE DAY 16

BLESSED BE YOUR NAME 24

BREATHE 20

COME, NOW IS THE TIME TO WORSHIP 29

DRAW ME CLOSE 32

ENOUGH 36

EVERLASTING GOD 40

FOREVER 44

GOD OF WONDERS 50

GREAT IS THY FAITHFULNESS 54

THE HEART OF WORSHIP 58

HERE I AM TO WORSHIP 47

HE'S ALWAYS BEEN FAITHFUL 62

HOLY IS THE LORD 66

HOSANNA (PRAISE IS RISING) 70

HOW CAN I KEEP FROM SINGING 74

HOW DEEP THE FATHER'S LOVE FOR US . . .86

HOW GREAT IS OUR GOD 78

HOW GREAT THOU ART 82

HUNGRY (FALLING ON MY KNEES) 89

IN CHRIST ALONE (MY HOPE IS FOUND) . . .92

JESUS, MESSIAH 98

LORD, I LIFT YOUR NAME ON HIGH 95

MARY, DID YOU KNOW? 102

OPEN THE EYES OF MY HEART 106

YOU ARE MY ALL IN ALL 116

YOU ARE MY KING (AMAZING LOVE) 110

YOU NEVER LET GO 119

YOUR GRACE IS ENOUGH 124

Produced by Alfred Music Publishing Co., Inc.
All rights reserved.   Printed in U.S.A.
ISBN-10: 0-7390-7428-8
ISBN-13: 978-0-7390-7428-2

Alfred

(Approx. Performance Time – 2:15)

ABOVE ALL

Words and Music by
Paul Baloche and Lenny LeBlanc
Arr. Victor Labenske

(Approx. Performance Time – 2:30)

ALL WHO ARE THIRSTY

Words and Music by
Brenton Brown and Glenn Robertson
Arr. Victor Labenske

(Approx. Performance Time – 2:15)

Amazing Grace (My Chains Are Gone)

Words and Music by
Chris Tomlin and Louie Giglio
Arr. Victor Labenske

BEAUTIFUL ONE

Words and Music by Tim Hughes
Arr. Victor Labenske

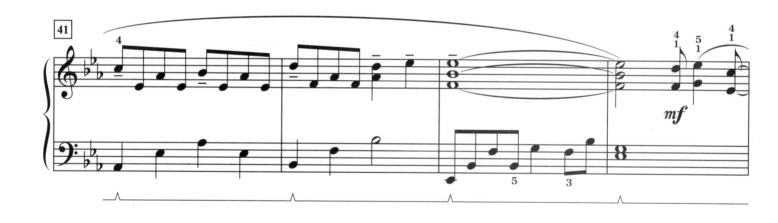

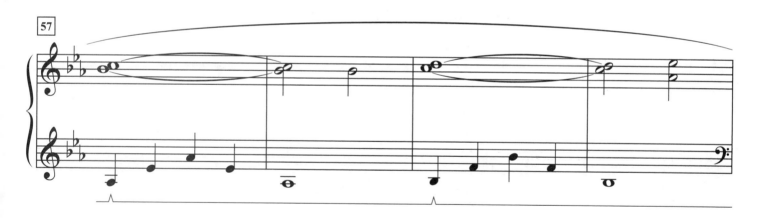

(Approx. Performance Time – 2:15)

Better Is One Day

Words and Music by Matt Redman
Arr. Victor Labenske

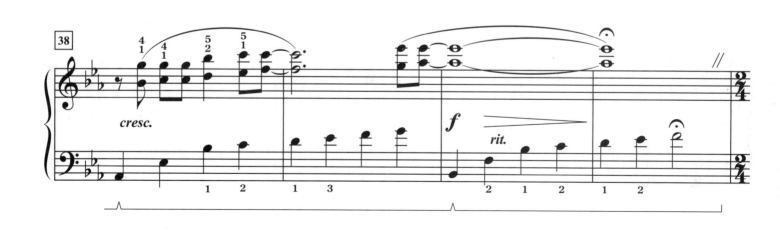

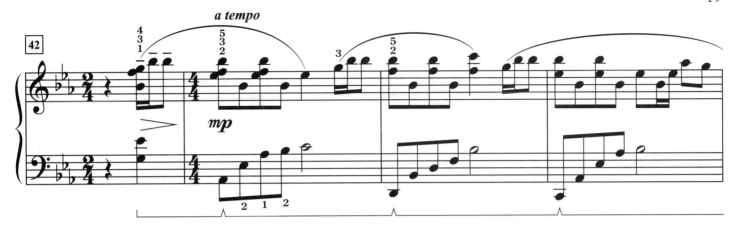

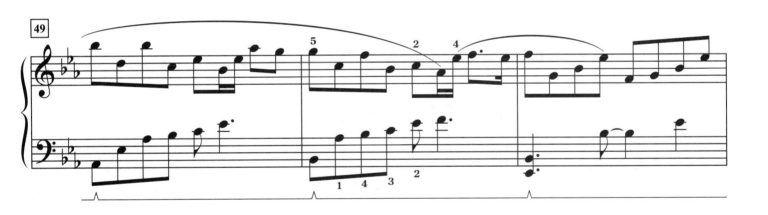

(Approx. Performance Time – 3:00)

BREATHE

Words and Music by Marie Barnett
Arr. Victor Labenske

(Approx. Performance Time – 3:00)

Blessed Be Your Name

Words and Music by
Beth Redman and Matt Redman
Arr. Victor Labenske

(Approx. Performance Time – 1:45)

COME, NOW IS THE TIME TO WORSHIP

Words and Music by Brian Doerksen
Arr. Victor Labenske

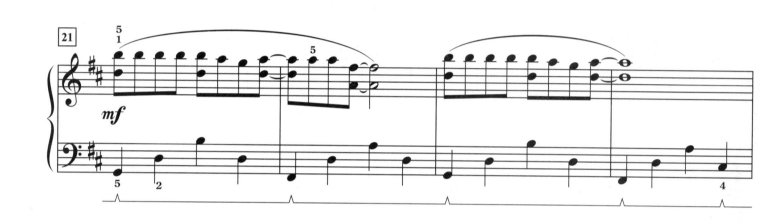

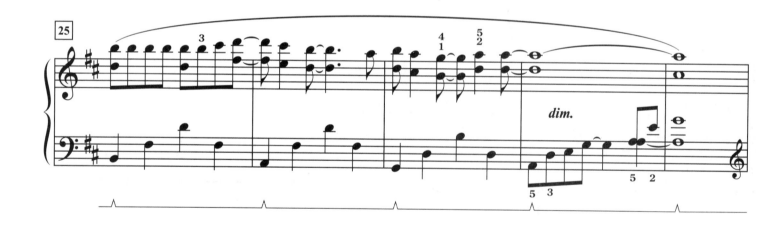

(Approx. Performance Time – 3:00)

DRAW ME CLOSE

Words and Music by Kelly Carpenter
Arr. Victor Labenske

(Approx. Performance Time – 2:15)

Enough

Words and Music by
Chris Tomlin and Louie Giglio
Arr. Victor Labenske

(Approx. Performance Time – 2:30)

Everlasting God

Words and Music by
Brenton Brown and Ken Riley
Arr. Victor Labenske

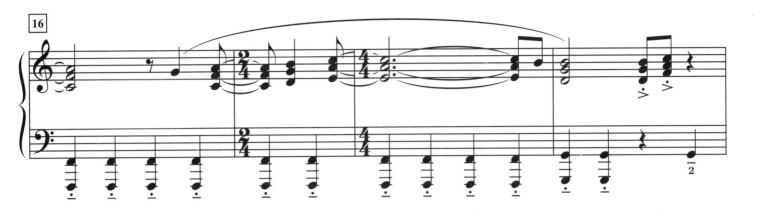

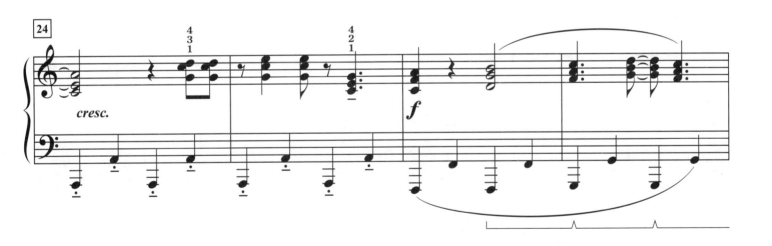

(Approx. Performance Time – 1:45)

FOREVER

Words and Music by Chris Tomlin
Arr. Victor Labenske

(Approx. Performance Time – 2:45)

Here I Am to Worship

Words and Music by Tim Hughes
Arr. Victor Labenske

(Approx. Performance Time – 2:45)

GOD OF WONDERS

Words and Music by
Marc Byrd and Steve Hindalong
Arr. Victor Labenske

(Approx. Performance Time – 3:00)

Great Is Thy Faithfulness

Words by Thomas O. Chisholm
Music by William M. Runyan
Arr. Victor Labenske

to E♭ Major chord

(Approx. Performance Time – 2:45)

THE HEART OF WORSHIP

Words and Music by Matt Redman
Arr. Victor Labenske

(Approx. Performance Time – 2:30)

He's Always Been Faithful

Words and Music by Sara Groves,
based upon "Great Is Thy Faithfulness" by
Thomas O. Chisholm and William M. Runyan
Arr. Victor Labenske

(Approx. Performance Time – 3:00)

Holy Is the Lord

Words and Music by
Chris Tomlin and Louie Giglio
Arr. Victor Labenske

(Approx. Performance Time – 3:00)

Hosanna (Praise Is Rising)

Words and Music by
Brenton Brown and Paul Baloche
Arr. Victor Labenske

(Approx. Performance Time – 3:15)

How Can I Keep from Singing

Words and Music by
Chris Tomlin, Ed Cash and Matt Redman
Arr. Victor Labenske

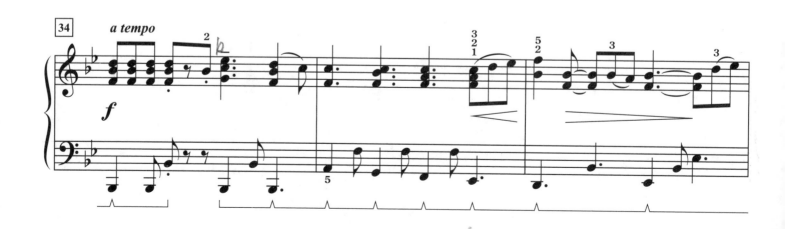

(Approx. Performance Time – 2:45)

How Great Is Our God

Words and Music by
Jesse Reeves, Chris Tomlin and Ed Cash
Arr. Victor Labenske

How Great Thou Art

Words and Music by Stuart K. Hine
Arr. Victor Labenske

(Approx. Performance Time – 3:00)

How Deep the Father's Love for Us

Words and Music by Stuart Townend
Arr. Victor Labenske

(Approx. Performance Time – 2:00)

HUNGRY (FALLING ON MY KNEES)

Words and Music by Kathryn Scott
Arr. Victor Labenske

(Approx. Performance Time – 2:30)

In Christ Alone (My Hope Is Found)

Words and Music by
Stuart Townend and Keith Getty
Arr. Victor Labenske

(Approx. Performance Time – 2:00)

Lord, I Lift Your Name on High

Words and Music by Rick Founds
Arr. Victor Labenske

(Approx. Performance Time – 3:00)

Jesus, Messiah

Words and Music by
Daniel Carson, Chris Tomlin, Ed Cash and Jesse Reeves
Arr. Victor Labenske

(Approx. Performance Time – 2:00)

Mary, Did You Know?

Words and Music by
Mark Lowry and Buddy Greene
Arr. Victor Labenske

(Approx. Performance Time – 2:30)

OPEN THE EYES OF MY HEART

Words and Music by Paul Baloche
Arr. Victor Labenske

(Approx. Performance Time – 2:30)

YOU ARE MY KING (AMAZING LOVE)

Words and Music by Billy James Foote
Arr. Victor Labenske

(Approx. Performance Time – 2:30)

You Are My All in All

Words and Music by Dennis L. Jernigan
Arr. Victor Labenske

(Approx. Performance Time – 2:30)

You Never Let Go

Words and Music by
Matt Redman and Beth Redman
Arr. Victor Labenske

(Approx. Performance Time – 2:45)

Your Grace Is Enough

Words and Music by Matt Maher
Arr. Victor Labenske